Map Skills

Written by
Renee Cummings

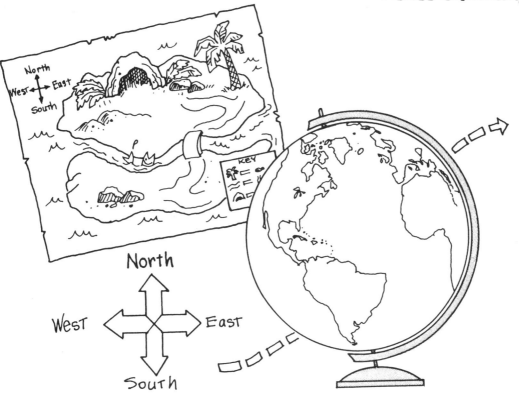

Cover Design
by
Matthew Van Zomeren

Inside Illustrations
by
Pat Biggs

Publishers
Instructional Fair • TS Denison
Grand Rapids, Michigan 49544

Permission to Reproduce

About the Book

Go beyond memorizing names and borders. Explore new routes to learning about maps. *Map Skills - Grade 2* journeys from reviewing the globe and compass rose to using a map scale and locating countries within continents. Your students will experience numerous and varied adventures using map symbols, map keys, and map scales as they follow the ice-cream truck, help Sam Super Spy complete a secret mission, go the distance in a bike-a-thon, and even travel across the United States to join some children on exciting vacations.

Every page offers opportunities for discussion. Work together as a class or with partners, and/or let the individual student work alone. Whether you use this book as your map study program or as a supplement to the social studies text, may you and your students have fun learning and exploring!

Credits

Author: Renee Cummings
Cover Design: Matthew Van Zomeren
Inside Illustrations: Pat Biggs
Project Director/Editor: Rhonda DeWaard
Editors: Sue Vanderlaan, Lisa Hancock
Typesetting/Layout: Pat Geasler

About the Author

Renee Cummings is an experienced author, having already written several books for Instructional Fair • TS Denison. She holds a Bachelor's Degree in Elementary Education from Oregon State University. Her 18 years of classroom experience include teaching remedial reading and various elementary grade levels.

Cover Art Elements – ©GlobeShots™, ©Cartesia Software, ©Visual Language

Standard Book Number: 1-56822-637-3
Map Skills - Grade 2
Copyright © 1998 by Instructional Fair • TS Denison
2400 Turner Avenue NW
Grand Rapids, Michigan 49544

Table of Contents

It's a Round World (*introducing the globe*) 4-5

A Global Guide (*the compass rose*) 6

Look to the Sky (*using directions*) 7

Dinosaur Fun Land (*using a map key*) 8

Awesome Aquarium (*using a map key*) 9-10

Carmella's Candy (*using map symbols*) 11

Bake Sale (*using map symbols*) 12

Back in Time (*using the compass rose*) 13

A Great Camp! (*making a map*) 14

Fantastic Seats! (*locating places on a floor plan*) 15

Science Sense (*using a floor plan and key*) 16

Prepare for the Show (*making a floor plan*) 17-18

Sign Search (*marking a route*) 19

To the Slopes (*following routes*) 20

Secret Mission (*marking routes*) 21-22

Find It There (*introducing a street map*) 23

At the Corner (*introduction to corners on a street map*) 24

Just a Few Blocks (*using a street map to follow routes*) 25

You're Invited (*using a street map and compass rose*) 26

Ice Cream! (*marking a route*) 27-28

Places to Go (*using a street map*) 29

Go the Distance (*introducing a map scale*) 30

Are We There Yet? (*using a map scale*) 31

Hot Air Balloon Race (*using a map scale*) 32

Across the Line (*boundary lines*) 33-34

Crossing the States (*using a compass rose on a United States map*) 35

Water Watch (*locating water on a map*) 36-37

What a Vacation! (*using a United States map*) 38-39

Where in the World? (*locating continents and oceans*) 40-42

Within Continents (*identifying countries*) 43-44

Answer Key 45-48

It's a Round World

Name _____

Use these maps with pages 5 and 6.

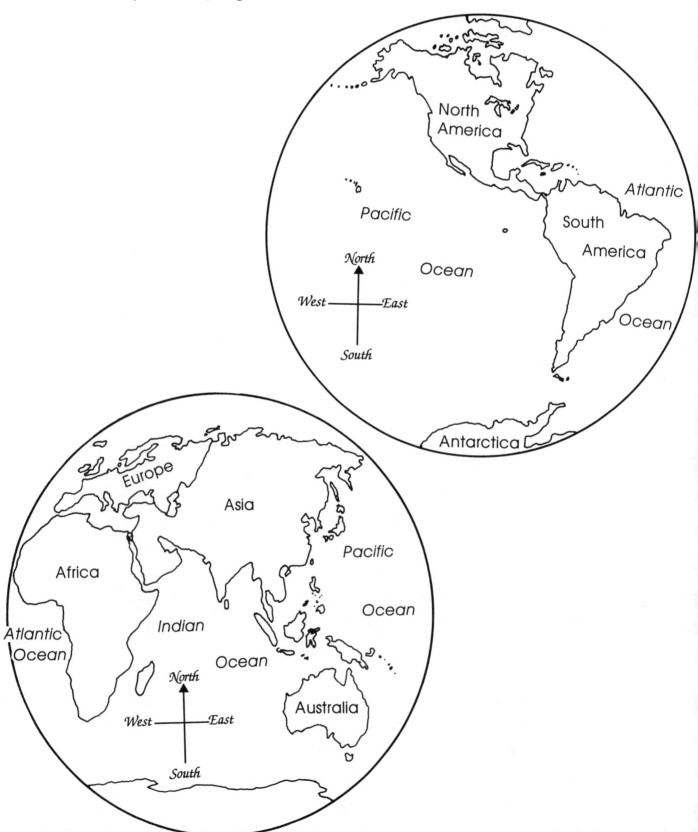

 It's a Round World (Continued)   Name _____

A globe is a map of the world that is shaped like a ball. The picture of the globe on page 4 shows both halves of the world. It shows the large pieces of land called continents. There are seven continents. Find them on the globe.

Write the names of the seven continents.

1. _____

2. _____

3. _____

4. _____

5. _____

6. _____

7. _____

There are three large bodies of water called oceans. Find the oceans on the globe. Write the names of the three oceans.

1. _____

2. _____

3. _____

 A Global Guide   Name _____

Use the globe pictures on page 4. Read the clues below. Write the answers on the lines. Then use the numbered letters to solve the riddle at the bottom of the page.

1. This direction points up.

___ ___ ___ ___ ___
  1   2   3

2. This direction points down.

___ ___ ___ ___ ___
4   5   6

3. This direction points right.

___ ___ ___ ___
7   8

4. This direction points left.

___ ___ ___ ___
9   10

5. This ocean is west of North America.

___ ___ ___ ___ ___ ___ ___
11 12

___ ___ ___ ___ ___
13   14

6. This ocean is south of Asia.

___ ___ ___ ___ ___ ___
15   16   17

___ ___ ___ ___ ___

7. This ocean is east of South America.

___ ___ ___ ___ ___ ___ ___
  18 19

___ ___ ___ ___ ___
20   21

Riddle: What does a globe do? ___ ___   ___ ___ ___ ___ ___ ___
                                    15 6   4   3 20 9   8

___ ___ " ___ _ ___ ___ ___ ___ "
5   10   12   2 1   5 21 16

___ ___ ___   ___ ___ ___ ___ ___ ___ .
13 5   2   11 19 14 17 7 18

 Look to the Sky

Name _____

Mr. McGill took his students on a field trip to the airport. A boy in his class drew this map of things they saw.

Airport Map

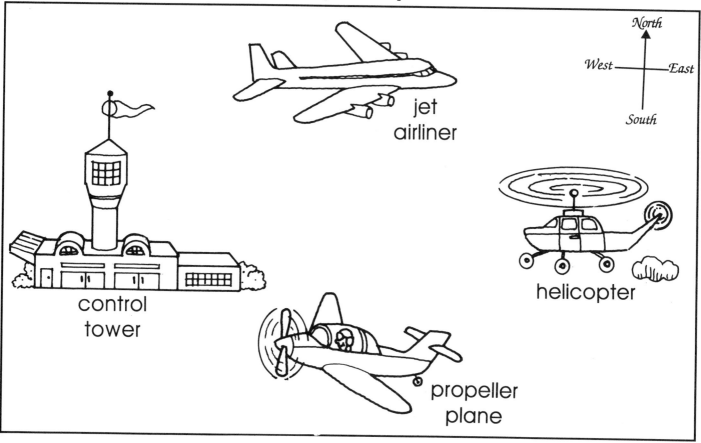

Write **north**, **south**, **west**, or **east** to complete each sentence.

1. Look _____ to see the jet airliner.

2. Look _____ to see the control tower.

3. Look _____ to see the propeller plane.

4. Look _____ to see the helicopter.

Dinosaur Fun Land

Name _____

Look at this map of Dinosaur Fun Land. A map key has pictures called symbols. The key tells what each symbol stands for on the map. Look at the key. Find each of the symbols on the map.

Dinosaur Fun Land Map

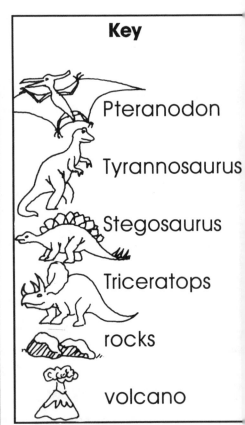

Key

Pteranodon

Tyrannosaurus

Stegosaurus

Triceratops

rocks

volcano

1. Color the Stegosaurus green.

2. Color the Tyrannosaurus blue.

3. Color the volcano red.

4. Color the Pteranodon orange.

5. Draw an **X** on the dinosaur that is below the Stegosaurus.

🌐 Awesome Aquarium

Name _____

Follow the directions on page 10 to complete this map.

Aquarium Map

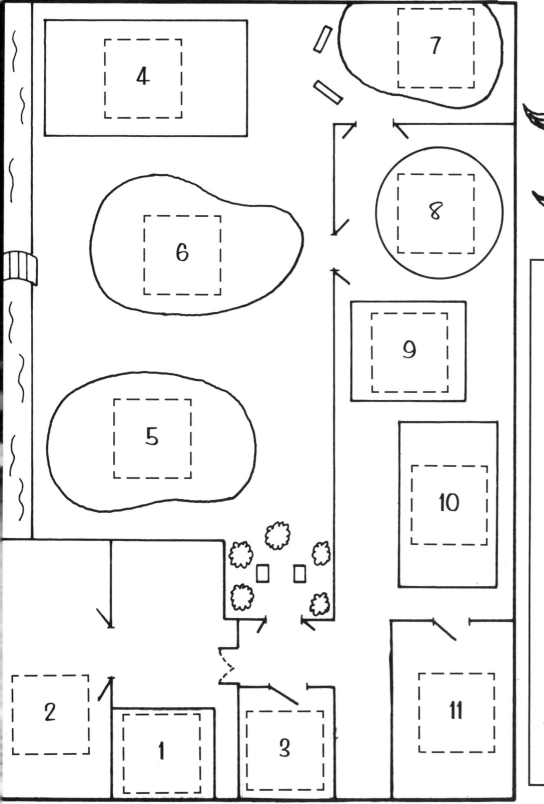

Key

1	Ticket Office
2	restaurant
3	gift shop
4	whale
5	otter
6	seal
7	puffin
8	octopus
9	jellyfish
10	tropical fish
11	movie room

Awesome Aquarium (Continued)   Name _____

Help complete the map for the new aquarium. Color all of the symbols blue. Cut out the symbols along the dotted lines. Then paste each symbol where it belongs on the map.

Carmella's Candy

Name _____

Carmella made a map of her candy store so that her customers could easily find their favorite candy. Use the map and key to answer the questions.

Candy Store Map

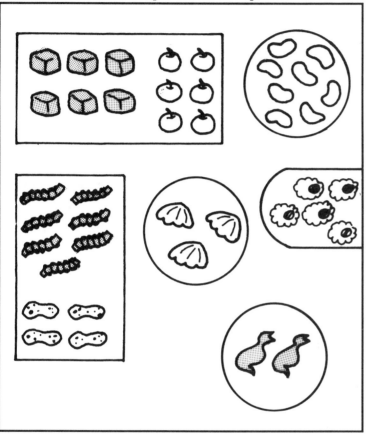

Key

1 symbol = 2 boxes of candy

chocolate chunks
cherry chocolates
licorice swirls
peanut clusters
cinnamon seashells
chewy dinosaurs
jelly beans
raspberry buttercreams

1. Each symbol equals how many boxes of candy? _____

2. How many boxes of each kind of candy are there?

jelly beans	_____	chocolate chunks	_____
peanut clusters	_____	raspberry buttercreams	_____
licorice swirls	_____	cherry chocolates	_____
chewy dinosaurs	_____	cinnamon seashells	_____

3. Carmella has the greatest number of boxes of which candy?

_____

_____

_____

 # Bake Sale

Name _____

Ms. Sweettooth's class is having a bake sale to raise money to go on a field trip. She drew a map of where each kind of baked item should be placed. Use the map key and symbols to answer the questions.

Bake Sale Map

1. Which baked item will be on the biggest table?

   _____

   _____

2. How many places are there for the people to pay for what

   they buy? _____

3. Where will the pies be placed? Color the table blue.

4. Where will the brownies be placed? Color the table brown.

5. Where will the cupcakes be placed? Color the table yellow.

6. Where will the cookies be placed? Color the table orange.

 Back in Time

Name _____

This is a map of a fort on the American frontier. Use the key, map and compass rose. Write the words **north, south, east,** and **west** to tell where the rooms are located in the fort.

Fort Map

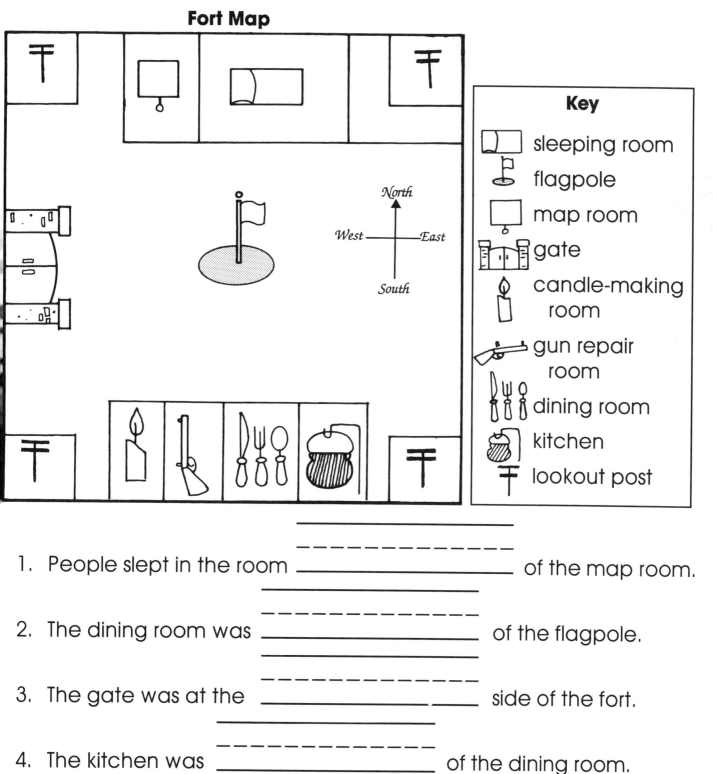

Key

sleeping room

flagpole

map room

gate

candle-making room

gun repair room

dining room

kitchen

lookout post

1. People slept in the room _____ of the map room.

2. The dining room was _____ of the flagpole.

3. The gate was at the _____ side of the fort.

4. The kitchen was _____ of the dining room.

 A Great Camp!

Name _____

Read the letter. Then draw a map to show what the camp looks like.
Make a key for the map.

June 20, 1988

Dear Elizabeth,

This camp is great! I'll tell you what is here.

There is a big wooden gate as you come into the campground at the north end. At the south end there is a lake where we swim and ride in boats. We sleep in five tents on the west side. A big log cabin on the east side is where we eat. We make necklaces and other things under a big tree that is north of the tents. At night we sing songs and tell stories around a campfire south of the log cabin.

I hope you are having fun at home. See you soon.

Your friend,

Sandy

Camp Map

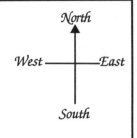

Key

Fantastic Seats!

Name _____

A floor plan can help you find your seat at a sports arena, concert hall, or any place where you may go to see a special event.

Read each ticket. Find the seat on the floor plan. Color the seat ( ) on the floor plan the correct color.

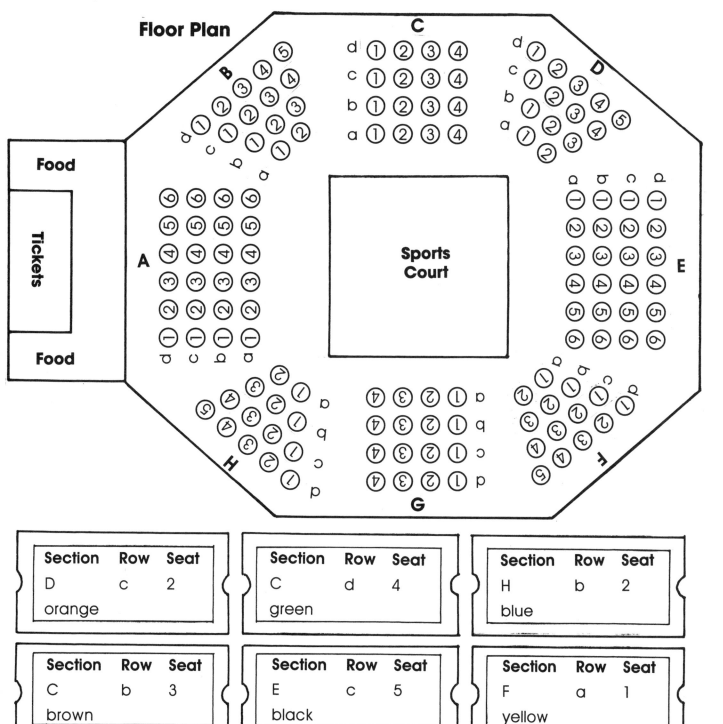

Section	Row	Seat
D	c	2
orange		

Section	Row	Seat
C	d	4
green		

Section	Row	Seat
H	b	2
blue		

Section	Row	Seat
C	b	3
brown		

Section	Row	Seat
E	c	5
black		

Section	Row	Seat
F	a	1
yellow		

Science Sense

Name _____

This is a floor plan of the Science Sense Museum. Use the floor plan and key to complete this page.

Museum Floor Plan

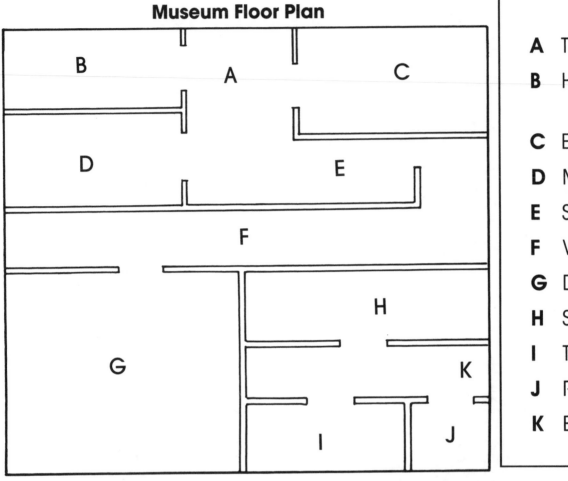

	Key
A	Ticket Gate
B	How Your Body Works
C	Electricity
D	Magnets
E	Solar System
F	Weather
G	Dinosaurs
H	Snack Bar
I	Tables
J	Restrooms
K	Exit Gate

1. In which room would you go to see dinosaurs? _____ Color the room brown.

2. In which room would you go to try using magnets? _____ Color the room blue.

3. Draw a hot dog in the snack bar.

4. Draw a table in the area in which tables are located.

5. Mark an **X** where you would buy a ticket to the museum.

6. If you go to room **E**, what will you learn about?

_____

- -

_____

Prepare for the Show

Name _____

It's the big event of the year! Old cars from all over the United States are being put on display. The boxes on the floor plan show the spaces where cars will be placed. Follow the directions on page 18 to complete the floor plan.

Car Display Floor Plan

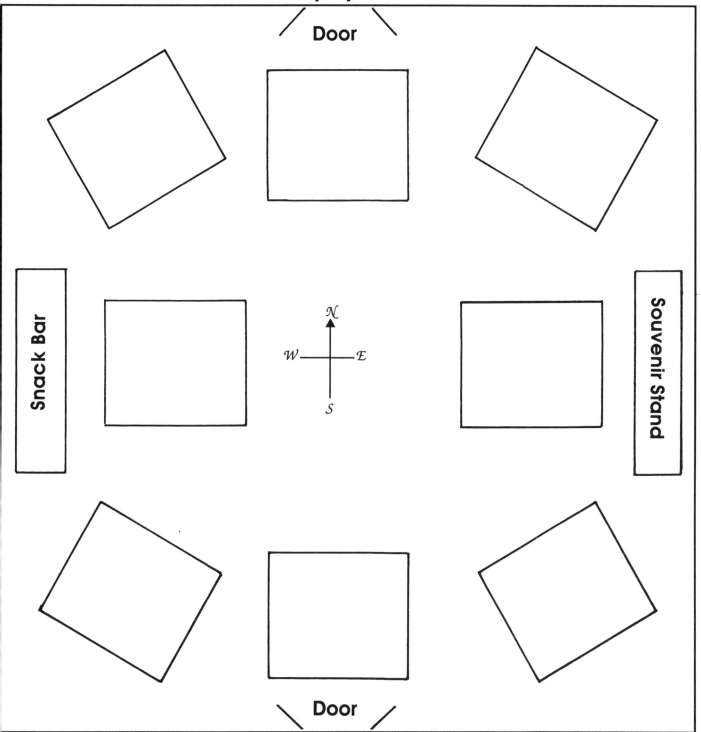

Prepare for the Show (Continued)   Name _____

Color and cut out the pictures of the cars at the bottom of the page. Read the directions below to paste the pictures where they belong on page 17.

1. The station wagon is in the space near the north door.

2. The roadster is in the space near the south door.

3. The van is in the space east of the station wagon.

4. The pickup is in the space west of the roadster.

5. The coupe is in the space west of the station wagon.

6. The carriage is in the space east of the roadster and south of the Souvenir Stand.

7. The Model A is east of the Snack Bar.

8. The Model T is east of the Model A.

 **Sign Search**

Name _____

Gina went for a hike. She found a piece of paper. There were strange directions written on it. Then she looked around and saw pictures drawn on the rocks in the area. Aha! The paper she had found was a route to follow. Read the directions and draw the route on the map.

Map

Key

corn
hunter
fish
river
buffalo
tree
arrowhead
cave

1. Start at the fish.

2. Go north to the corn.

3. Then go east to the hunter.

4. Go south to the river.

5. Go west to the buffalo.

6. Go south to the tree.

7. Go east to the arrowhead.

8. Go north to the cave. Draw a picture on the cave to show the treasure chest Gina finds there.

 # To the Slopes

Name _____

It's wintertime. Everyone wants to go sledding, skiing, or snowboarding on the slopes of Snow Peak Mountain. There are four different buses headed to the mountain. Each bus takes a different route. Use the map, map key, and compass rose to help you answer the questions.

1. Bus 4 drives the route that goes _____ _____ .

   It picks up people in the towns of _____ _____ _____ .

2. Mitzi lives in Great Pass. She will ride Bus Number _____ .

3. Greg lives in Portsville. He will ride Bus Number _____ .

4. Bailey lives in Garden Ridge. She will ride Bus Number _____ .

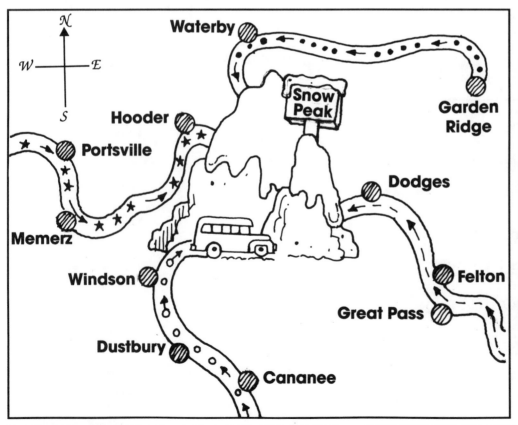

 Secret Mission

Name _____

Sam Super Spy is on a mission. He must get the secret papers and deliver them to his boss as soon as possible. This is a map of where the mission is to take place. Follow the directions on page 22 to help Sam.

Key

- bench
- river
- bridge
- path
- tree
- swing
- jungle gym
- fountain
- duck pond
- wastebasket
- entrance

Secret Mission (Continued)   Name _____

Use a red crayon to mark the route Sam will take.

1. Enter the park through the entrance at the north end of the park.

2. Turn and walk east and then south past the swings and jungle gym.

3. Turn and go west to the fountain.

4. Walk to the south side of the fountain.

5. Walk to the bench south of the fountain.

6. You will find the papers you want under the wastebasket to the west of the bench. Draw a red **X** on where Sam finds the secret papers.

Now Sam must deliver the secret papers to his boss. Use a blue crayon to mark the route Sam will take. Start at the red **X** you drew.

1. Walk south to the path.

2. Turn and walk east along the path to the wastebasket.

3. Turn and walk south near the duck pond.

4. Walk south to the path.

5. Turn and walk west toward the bridge.

6. There is a man standing under the tree north of the bridge. Sam hands the secret papers to him. Mission completed! Draw a blue **X** to show where Sam delivered the secret papers.

 Find It There

Name _____

To find your way around a town or city you can use a street map. It shows the names of the streets.

Find the bookstore on the key. Now find it on the map. Look at the name of the street that goes past the bookstore. If you want to go to the bookstore, you will have to go to Smelt Street.

Street Map

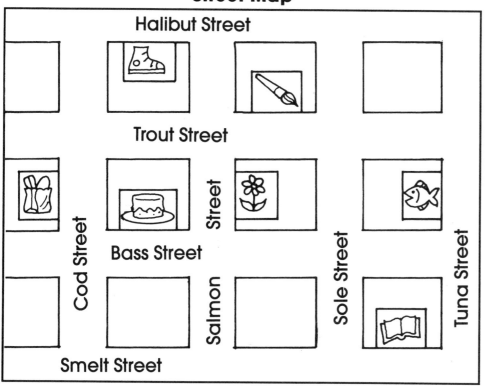

Use the street map and map key. Fill in the blanks.

1. You can buy a cake on _____ Street.

2. You can buy new shoes on _____ Street.

3. You can buy a new fish tank on _____ Street.

4. What store is on Salmon Street? _____

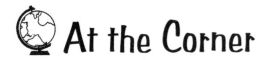 **At the Corner**

Name _____

A street map shows how a town or city is divided into blocks. The corners of blocks are made when two streets cross each other. Use the street map to answer the questions.

Street Map

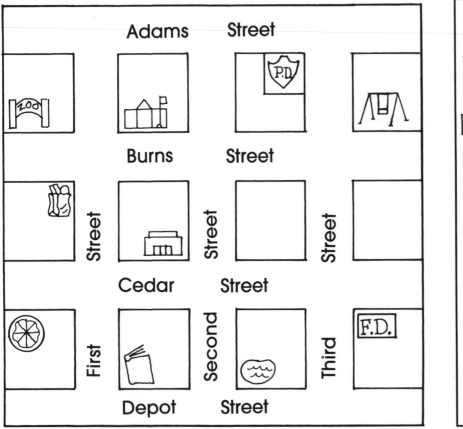

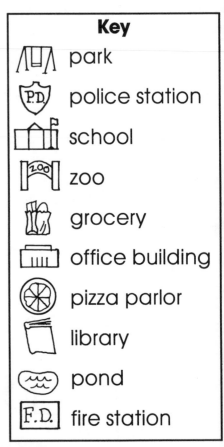

Key

park

police station

school

zoo

grocery

office building

pizza parlor

library

pond

fire station

1. What is at the corner of First Street and Burns Street?

   _____

   _____

2. What is at the corner of Second Street and Depot Street?

   _____

3. Circle the names of the two streets that cross each other to make the corner where you can find the . . .

   • park . . .   Adams Street   Burns Street   Third Street

   • grocery . . .   Burns Street   Cedar Street   First Street

Just a Few Blocks

Name _____

Street Map

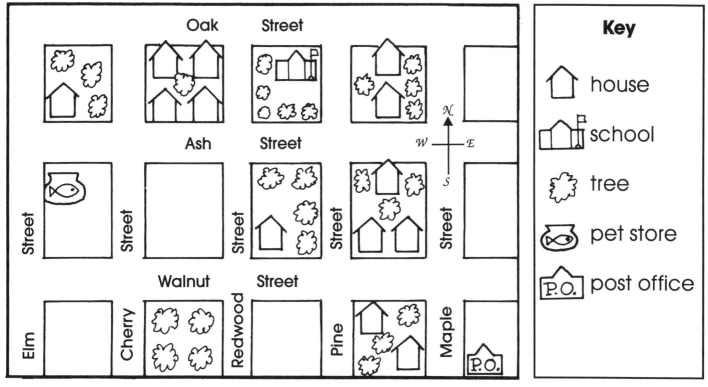

Hannah's class is going on a field trip to the post office. Read the route they walked. Use a blue crayon to draw the route on the map.

(1)   They leave the school and walk 1 block south.

(2)   Then they walk 1 block east.

(3)   Now they walk 2 blocks south.

The class will walk back to school along a different route. Read the route they walked. Use a red crayon to draw the route on the map.

(1)   They leave the post office and walk 1 block north.

(2)   Then they walk 3 blocks west.

(3)   Now they walk 2 blocks north.

(4)   Then they walk 2 blocks east.

Circle the route that was longer . . .

          going to the post office   returning to school

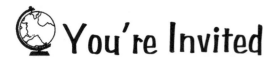 # You're Invited

Name _____

Liz sent out invitations to her birthday party. She drew a map to show how to go from school to her house. Write **north**, **south**, **east**, or **west** and the street name to complete the sentences.

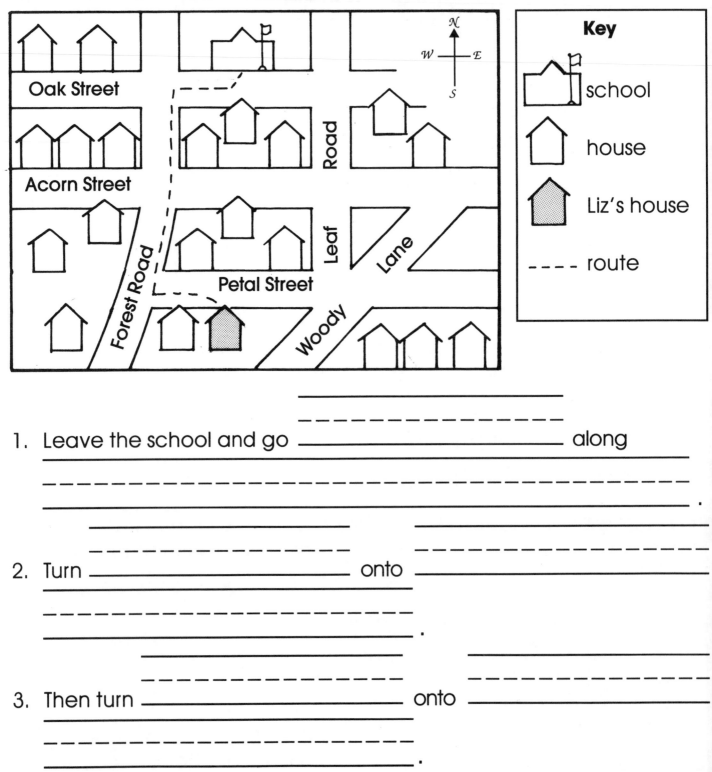

1. Leave the school and go _____ along
   _____ .

2. Turn _____ onto _____ .

3. Then turn _____ onto _____ .

 Ice Cream!

Name _____

Ding – Ding – Ding-a-ling! Here comes the ice-cream truck. On hot summer days, Stan drives his ice-cream truck around the neighborhood. He takes the same route every day. This map shows the neighborhood where Stan drives. Follow the directions on page 28.

Ice-Cream Route Map

Orange Swirl Street

Vanilla Lane

Strawberry Avenue

Rocky Road Avenue

Chocolate Road

Cookie Crunch Street

Butternut Road

Key

Stan's house

house

school

library

park

swimming pool

jogging track

tree

fire station

 Ice Cream! (Continued)

Name _____

Draw Stan's route on the map on page 27. To do this, read the information below. The map key and compass rose on page 27 will help you.

1. Stan backs out of his driveway onto Orange Swirl Street.

2. He goes east.

3. Then he turns south onto Strawberry Avenue.

4. He drives past the swimming pool. After he passes the jogging track, he turns west onto Vanilla Lane.

5. He drives around Vanilla Lane. Then he drives east on Butternut Road past the park.

6. He turns and drives north along Rocky Road Avenue.

7. At the corner he turns and drives east along Orange Swirl Street.

8. He passes the library and drives south along Chocolate Road.

9. He turns east onto Butternut Road and drives past the row of trees.

10. Then he turns north and drives along Cookie Crunch Street.

11. He passes the fire station and turns west and drives along Orange Swirl Street until he reaches his home.

 Places to Go

Name _____

Mrs. Nelson needs to do many errands this afternoon. She only has a short time in which to do everything. Read Mrs. Nelson's list of things to do. Use the street map, map key, and symbols to answer the questions.

Mrs. Nelson's Map

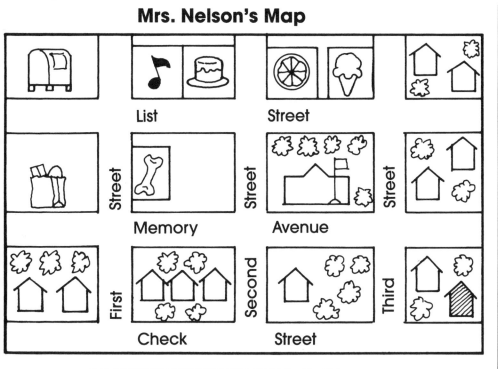

Things to Do

1. Pick up Tony and Erica at school
2. Buy new leash for Sassy
3. Mail package to Granny
4. Order cake for Dad's birthday
5. Pick up pizza for dinner

1. On the map, find the places Mrs. Nelson needs to go.

2. Mrs. Nelson will go to these places in the same order as her list of things to do. Write the number on each place on the map to show the order in which she will go to these places.

3. Start at Mrs. Nelson's house. Use a red crayon to draw the route Mrs. Nelson will take to do all of her errands.

 Go the Distance

Name _____

This map shows the route for the yearly Pedalville Bike-a-thon. At the bottom of the map is a scale. A map scale helps you measure distance on a map.

Bike-a-thon Map

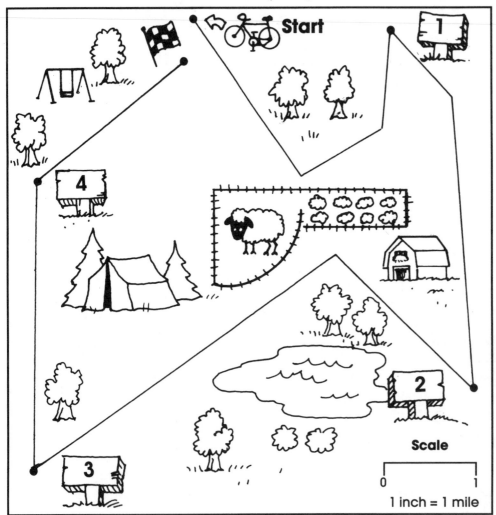

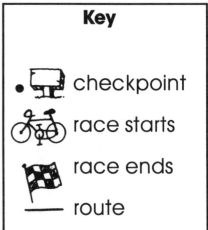

Key

• 🔲 checkpoint

🚲 race starts

🏁 race ends

—— route

Scale

0   1

1 inch = 1 mile

Use a ruler and the scale to measure the distances on the map.

1. How many miles are between "race starts" and checkpoint 1? _____

2. How many miles are between checkpoint 1 and checkpoint 2? _____

3. How many miles are between checkpoint 2 and checkpoint 3? _____

4. How many miles are between checkpoint 3 and checkpoint 4? _____

5. How many miles are between checkpoint 4 and "race ends"? _____

 Are We There Yet?

Name _____

Calvin is going on a vacation to Getaway Campground. Use the scale and a ruler to answer the questions below.

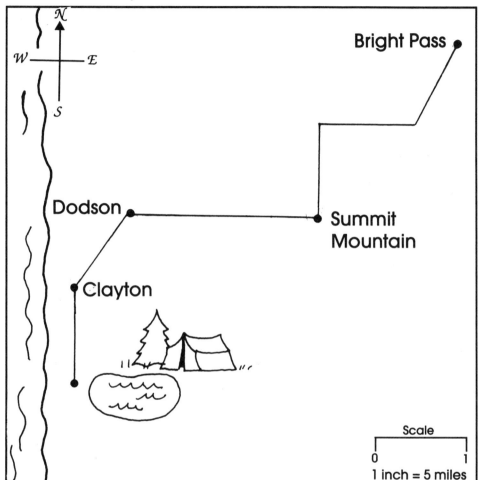

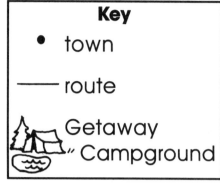

Key
- • town
- —— route
- Getaway Campground

Scale

0 _____ 1

1 inch = 5 miles

1. How many miles are there between Bright Pass and Summit Mountain? _____

2. How many miles are there between Dodson and Clayton? _____

3. How far is it from Clayton to Getaway Campground? _____

4. How far is it from Summit Mountain to Dodson? _____

5. How many miles in all are there between Bright Pass and Getaway Campground? _____

Hot Air Balloon Race

Name _____

It's the Grand Hot Air Balloon Race. Use the map scale and a ruler to find out how far the hot air balloons will travel each day of the race.

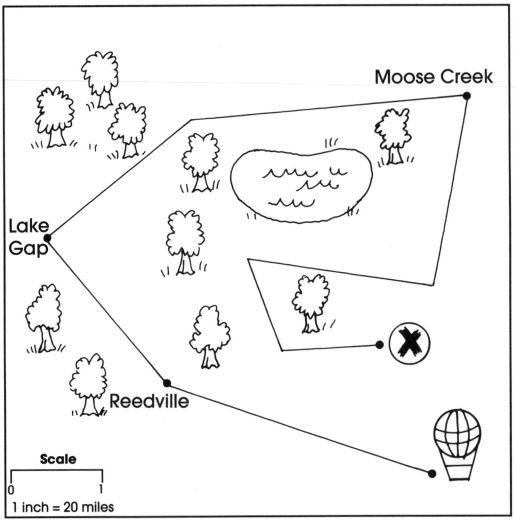

Key

🎈 race begins

• landing area

— flight path

Ⓧ finish circle

Scale
0 ———— 1
1 inch = 20 miles

1. On the first day of the Hot Air Balloon Race, the balloons will travel to Reedville. They will travel _____ miles.

2. The second day of the race, the balloons will travel from Reedville to Lake Gap. They will travel _____ miles.

3. On the third day of the race, the balloons will travel from Lake Gap to Moose Creek. They will travel _____ miles.

4. On the last day of the race, the balloons will travel from Moose Creek to the finish circle. They will travel _____ miles.

Across the Line

Name _____

This is a map of the United States. The lines show the boundaries of each state. Use this page with page 34 and page 35.

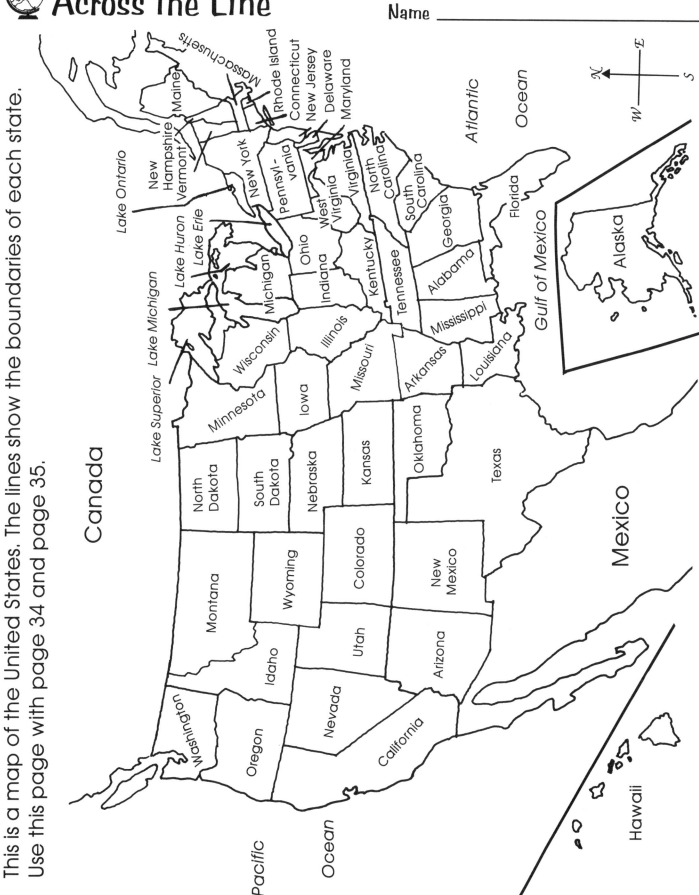

Across the Line (Continued)   Name _____

Use the United States map on page 33 to complete the following.

1. What is the name of the state in which you live?

   _____

   _____

2. Draw a blue line along the boundary lines of the state where
   you live.

3. What country is north of the United States?

   _____

   _____

4. Draw a green line along the boundary between the United States
   and Canada.

5. What country is south of the United States?

   _____

   _____

6. Draw an orange line along the southern boundary of the United
   States.

7. Find the state, country, or body of water that is the . . .

   northern boundary of your state. Color it green.

   eastern boundary of your state. Color it blue.

   southern boundary of your state. Color it yellow.

   western boundary of your state. Color it red.

Crossing the States

Name _____

Use the map of the United States on page 33 and the compass rose to fill in the puzzle.

Across

2. the state east of Indiana
6. the state west of North Dakota
8. the small state south of Massachusetts
10. the state south of Georgia
11. the state west of Utah

Down

1. the state west of New Hampshire
2. the state south of Washington
3. the state north of Missouri
4. the state east of Arizona
5. the larger state south of New York
7. the state north of South Dakota
9. the state south of Arkansas

Water Watch

Name _____

On this map of the United States, the rivers are shown with a - - - - . Use a blue crayon to trace along each of the rivers. Seven of the largest lakes are shown on the map. Find and color them blue. Then go on to page 37.

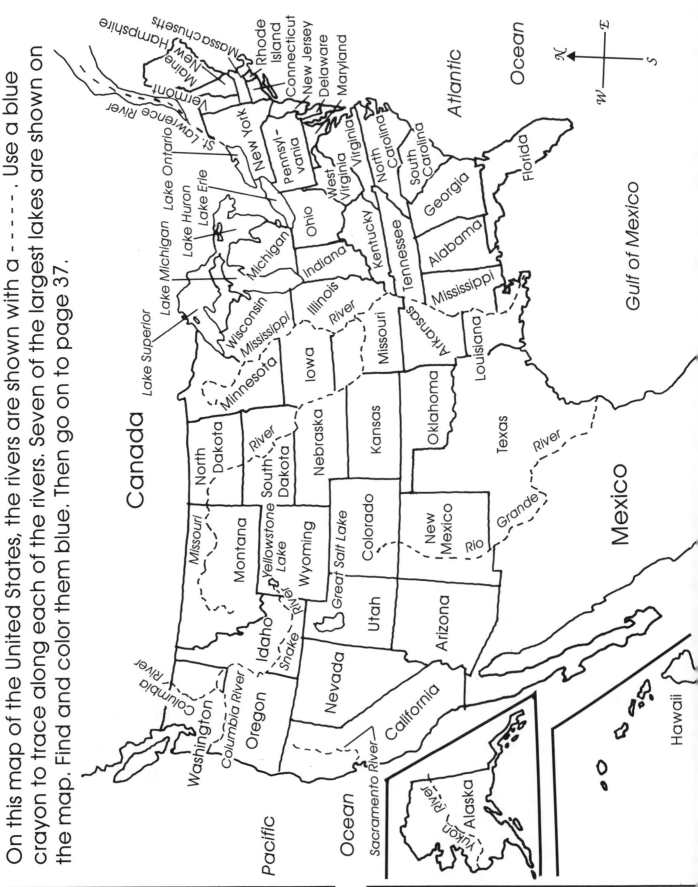

Water Watch (Continued)   Name _____

Use the map on page 36 to find the answers to the questions.

1. The lakes along the northern border of the United States are called the Great Lakes. Write the names of these five lakes.

_____

_____

_____

_____

_____

2. Which river flows along the border between Canada and the United States?

_____

_____

3. What is the name of the lake in Utah?

_____

_____

4. Which river flows along the border between Washington and Oregon?

_____

_____

5. Circle the name of the river that flows along the border between Mexico and the United States.

Mississippi River   Rio Grande River   Yukon River   Missouri River

6. Circle the name of the river that flows through the state of Alaska.

Mississippi River   Rio Grande River   Yukon River   Missouri River

7. How many states does the Mississippi River flow through or past?

_____

⊕ What a Vacation!

Name _____

This is a map of the United States. It shows where four children went for a vacation. Use this map and the key on page 39 to find out where each child went.

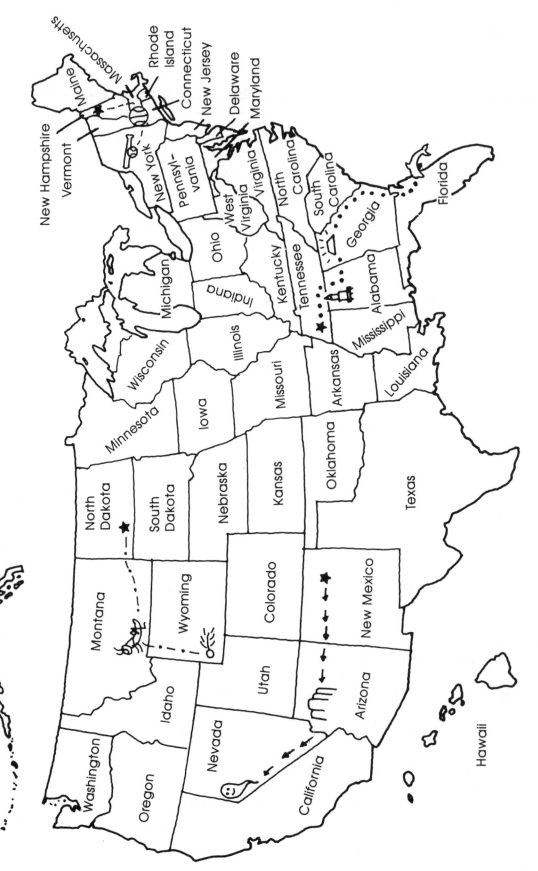

 **What a Vacation!** (Continued)

Name _____

Key

→ → →	David's trip		Dahlonega Gold Museum
• • • •	Becky's trip		Sea World
- - - -	Adam's trip		Grand Canyon
—·—·—	Sheila's trip		U.S. Space and Rocket Center
✳	home		Grasshopper Glacier
	National Baseball Hall of Fame and Museum		Basketball Hall of Fame
	Fossil Butte National Monument		Virginia City (old mining town)

1. Use a yellow crayon to trace David's route.

2. Use a blue crayon to trace Becky's route.

3. Use a red crayon to trace Adam's route.

4. Use a green crayon to trace Sheila's route.

5. Which person probably likes sports? _____

6. Which person traveled the farthest west? _____

7. Which person traveled the farthest south? _____

8. Write the names of the places Sheila went to see on her vacation.

_____

_____

9. Where did Becky go in Florida? _____

Where in the World?   Name _____

Refer to the globe pictures on page 4, a real globe, or a world map. Find the seven continents and three oceans. Now you are ready to make your own globe using this page and a copy of page 41 and 42.

1. Cut out all the continent and ocean labels.

2. Paste them where they belong in the boxes on the maps on pages 41 and 42 .

3. Color the continents green. Color the oceans blue. Be careful not to color the word labels.

4. Cut out all of the map circles along the outer lines.

5. Fold each circle in half along the dotted line. Keep the map side on the inside.

6. Be sure to keep the numbers on the circles at the top. Glue the back of the right half of circle 1 to the back of the left half of circle 2.

7. Glue the back of the right half of circle 2 to the back of the left half of circle 3.

8. Glue the back of the right half of circle 3 to the back of the left half of circle 4.

9. Complete the globe by gluing the back of the right half of circle 4 to the back of the left half of circle 1.

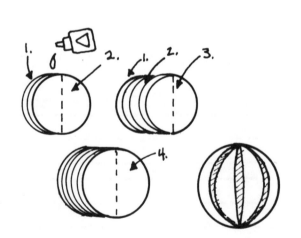

Keep your globe at your desk to help you to learn the continents and oceans of our world.

Where in the World? (Continued)

Name _____

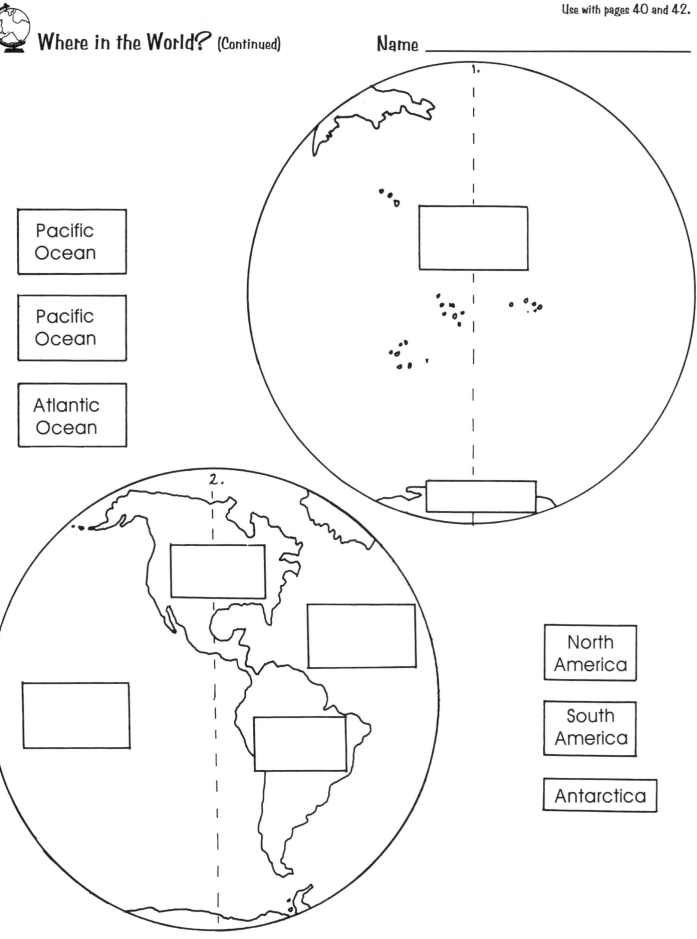

Pacific
Ocean

Pacific
Ocean

Atlantic
Ocean

North
America

South
America

Antarctica

Where in the World? (Continued)

Name _____

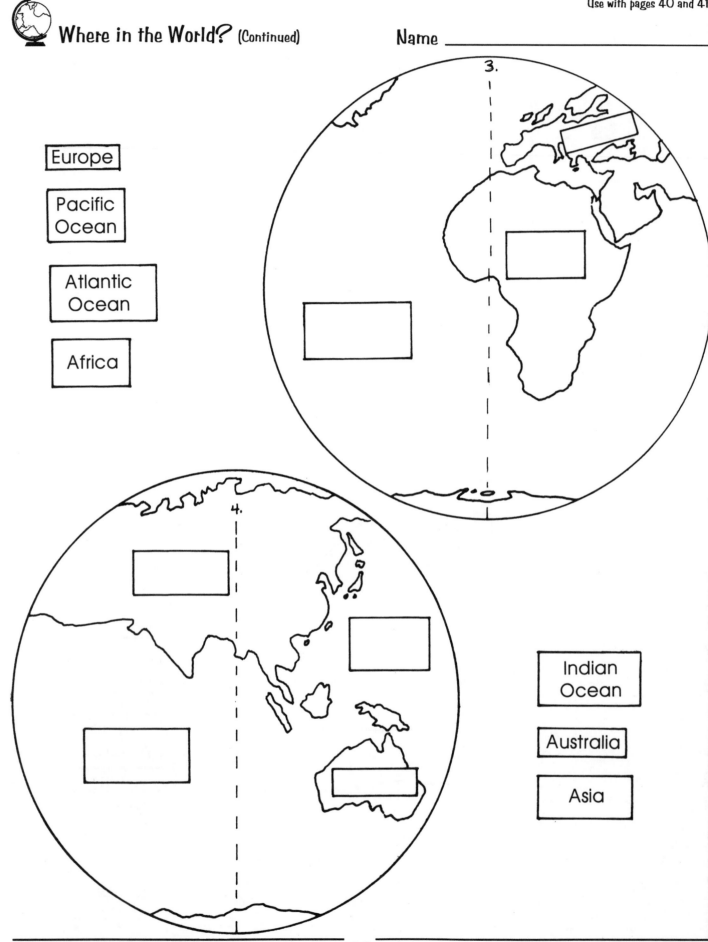

Europe

Pacific
Ocean

Atlantic
Ocean

Africa

Indian
Ocean

Australia

Asia

Within Continents

Name _____

This map shows two continents and two oceans. It also shows the countries that are on each continent. A solid line (————) shows the boundaries of each country. Use this map to answer the questions on page 44.

Within Continents (Continued)   Name _____

1. Write the names of the continents shown on the map.

    _____

    _____

    _____

    _____

    _____

2. Find the United States on the map. Color it green.

3. Find Alaska and Hawaii. They are part of the country of the United States. Color them green.

4. What country is north of the United States? Color it orange.

    _____

    _____

5. What large country is south of the United States. Color it red.

    _____

    _____

6. Which South American country is the biggest?

    _____

    _____

7. What long, skinny country is on the west coast of South America?

    _____

    _____

8. Which ocean is to the west of the continents of North America and South America?

    _____

    _____

9. In which direction would you go to travel from Canada to Chile?

    _____

    _____

Map Skills

Answer Key
Grade 2

It's a Round World (Continued)   Name _____

A globe is a map of the world that is shaped like a ball. The picture of the globe on page 4 shows both halves of the world. It shows the large pieces of land called continents. There are seven continents. Find them on the globe.

Write the names of the seven continents.

1. North America
2. South America
3. Antarctica
4. Asia
5. Europe
6. Africa
7. Australia

There are three large bodies of water called oceans. Find the oceans on the globe. Write the names of the three oceans.

1. Atlantic Ocean
2. Pacific Ocean
3. Indian Ocean

Page 5

A Global Guide   Name _____

Use the globe pictures on page 4. Read the clues below. Write the answers on the lines. Then use the numbered letters to solve the riddle at the bottom of the page.

1. This direction points up.   n o r t h
2. This direction points down.   s o u t h
3. This direction points right.   e a s t
4. This direction points left.   w e s t
5. This ocean is west of North America.   P a c i f i c   O c e a n
6. This ocean is south of Asia.   I n d i a n   O c e a n
7. This ocean is east of South America.   A t l a n t i c   O c e a n

Riddle: What does a globe do?   I t   s h o w s   u s   a   r o u n d   o u r   p l a n e t

Page 6

Look to the Sky   Name _____

Mr. McGill took his students on a field trip to the airport. A boy in his class drew this map of things they saw.

Airport Map

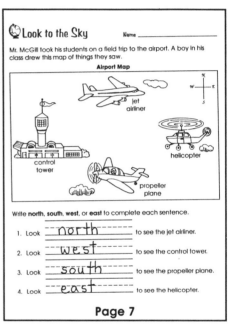

Write **north**, **south**, **west**, or **east** to complete each sentence.

1. Look ___north___ to see the jet airliner.
2. Look ___west___ to see the control tower.
3. Look ___south___ to see the propeller plane.
4. Look ___east___ to see the helicopter.

Page 7

Dinosaur Fun Land   Name _____

Look at this map of Dinosaur Fun Land. A map key has pictures called symbols. The key tells what each symbol stands for on the map. Look at the key. Find each of the symbols on the map.

Dinosaur Fun Land Map

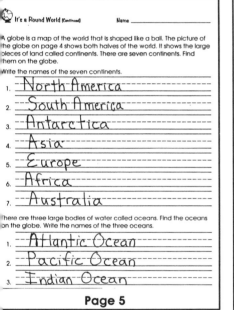

1. Color the Stegosaurus green.
2. Color the Tyrannosaurus blue.
3. Color the volcano red.
4. Color the Pteranodon orange.
5. Draw an **X** on the dinosaur that is below the Stegosaurus.

Page 8

Awesome Aquarium   Name _____

Follow the directions on page 10 to complete this map.

Aquarium Map

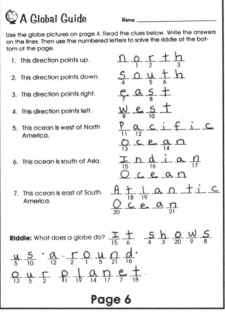

Page 9

Carmella's Candy   Name _____

Carmella made a map of her candy store so that her customers could easily find their favorite candy. Use the map and key to answer the questions.

Candy Store Map

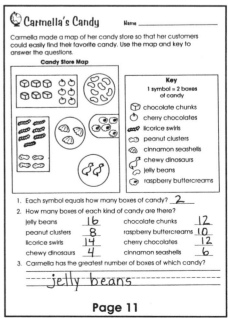

1. Each symbol equals how many boxes of candy?   2
2. How many boxes of each kind of candy are there?

jelly beans	16	chocolate chunks	12
peanut clusters	8	raspberry buttercreams	10
licorice swirls	14	cherry chocolates	12
chewy dinosaurs	4	cinnamon seashells	6

3. Carmella has the greatest number of boxes of which candy?

   jelly beans

Page 11

Bake Sale

Name _____

Ms. Sweettooth's class is having a bake sale to raise money to go on a field trip. She drew a map of where each kind of baked item should be placed. Use the map key and symbols to answer the questions.

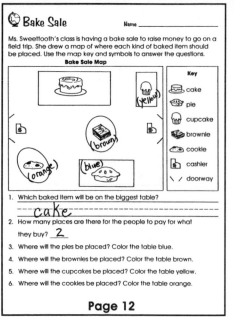

Bake Sale Map

Key
- cake
- pie
- cupcake
- brownie
- cookie
- cashier
- doorway

1. Which baked item will be on the biggest table?

   _____cake_____

2. How many places are there for the people to pay for what they buy? __2__

3. Where will the pies be placed? Color the table blue.

4. Where will the brownies be placed? Color the table brown.

5. Where will the cupcakes be placed? Color the table yellow.

6. Where will the cookies be placed? Color the table orange.

Page 12

Back in Time

Name _____

This is a map of a fort on the American frontier. Use the key, map and compass rose. Write the words **north**, **south**, **east**, and **west** to tell where the rooms are located in the fort.

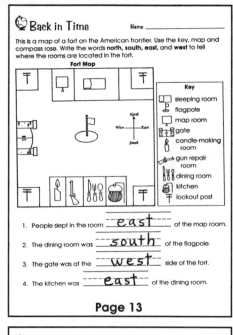

Fort Map

Key
- sleeping room
- flagpole
- map room
- gate
- candle-making room
- gun repair room
- dining room
- kitchen
- lookout post

1. People slept in the room __east__ of the map room.

2. The dining room was __south__ of the flagpole.

3. The gate was at the __west__ side of the fort.

4. The kitchen was __east__ of the dining room.

Page 13

A Great Camp!

Name _____

Read the letter. Then draw a map to show what the camp looks like. Make a key for the map.

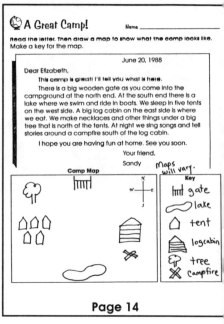

June 20, 1988

Dear Elizabeth,

This camp is great! I'll tell you what is here.

There is a big wooden gate as you come into the campground at the north end. At the south end there is a lake where we swim and ride in boats. We sleep in five tents on the west side. A big log cabin on the east side is where we eat. We make necklaces and other things under a big tree that is north of the tents. At night we sing songs and tell stories around a campfire south of the log cabin.

I hope you are having fun at home. See you soon.

Your friend,

Sandy

Maps will vary.

Camp Map

Key
- gate
- lake
- tent
- logcabin
- tree
- campfire

Page 14

Fantastic Seats!

Name _____

A floor plan can help you find your seat at a sports arena, concert hall, or any place where you may go to see a special event.

Read each ticket. Find the seat on the floor plan. Color the seat ( ) on the floor plan the correct color.

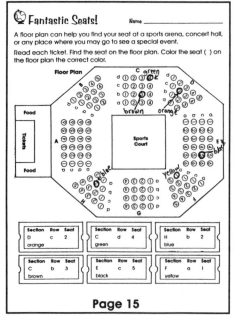

Floor Plan

Section	Row	Seat
D orange	c	2

Section	Row	Seat
C green	d	4

Section	Row	Seat
H blue	b	2

Section	Row	Seat
C brown	b	3

Section	Row	Seat
E black	c	5

Section	Row	Seat
F yellow	a	1

Page 15

Science Sense

Name _____

This is a floor plan of the Science Sense Museum. Use the floor plan and key to complete this page.

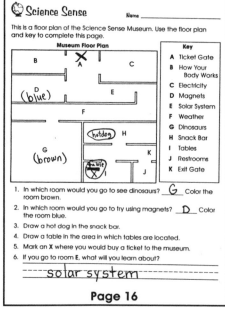

Museum Floor Plan

Key
- A Ticket Gate
- B How Your Body Works
- C Electricity
- D Magnets
- E Solar System
- F Weather
- G Dinosaurs
- H Snack Bar
- I Tables
- J Restrooms
- K Exit Gate

1. In which room would you go to see dinosaurs? __G__ Color the room brown.

2. In which room would you go to try using magnets? __D__ Color the room blue.

3. Draw a hot dog in the snack bar.

4. Draw a table in the area in which tables are located.

5. Mark an X where you would buy a ticket to the museum.

6. If you go to room E, what will you learn about?

   _____solar system_____

Page 16

Prepare for the Show

Name _____

It's the big event of the year! Old cars from all over the United States are being put on display. The boxes on the floor plan show the spaces where cars will be placed. Follow the directions on page 18 to complete the floor plan.

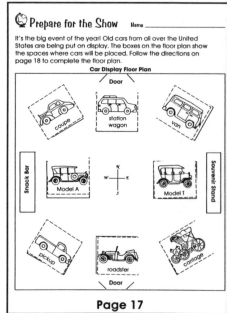

Car Display Floor Plan

Door

- coupe
- station wagon
- van
- Snack Bar
- Model A
- Model T
- Souvenir Stand
- pickup
- roadster
- carriage

Door

Page 17

Sign Search

Name _____

Gina went for a hike. She found a piece of paper. There were strange directions written on it. Then she looked around and saw pictures drawn on the rocks in the area. Aha! The paper she had found was a route to follow. Read the directions and draw the route on the map.

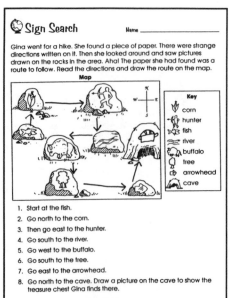

Map

Key
- corn
- hunter
- fish
- river
- buffalo
- tree
- arrowhead
- cave

1. Start at the fish.
2. Go north to the corn.
3. Then go east to the hunter.
4. Go south to the river.
5. Go west to the buffalo.
6. Go north to the tree.
7. Go east to the arrowhead.
8. Go north to the cave. Draw a picture on the cave to show the treasure chest Gina finds there.

Page 19

To the Slopes

Name _____

It's wintertime. Everyone wants to go sledding, skiing, or snowboarding on the slopes of Snow Peak Mountain. There are four different buses headed to the mountain. Each bus takes a different route. Use the map, map key, and compass rose to help you answer the questions.

1. Bus 4 drives the route that goes _____north_____

   It picks up people in the towns of _____Cananee,_____

   _____Dustbury, Windson_____

2. Mitzi lives in Great Pass. She will ride Bus Number __2__.
3. Greg lives in Portsville. He will ride Bus Number __3__.
4. Bailey lives in Garden Ridge. She will ride Bus Number __1__.

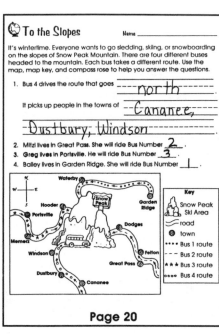

Key
- Snow Peak Ski Area
- road
- town
- • • • Bus 1 route
- - - - Bus 2 route
- ★ ★ Bus 3 route
- ◦ ◦ ◦ Bus 4 route

Page 20

Secret Mission

Name _____

Sam Super Spy is on a mission. He must get the secret papers and deliver them to his boss as soon as possible. This is a map of where the mission is to take place. Follow the directions on page 22 to help Sam.

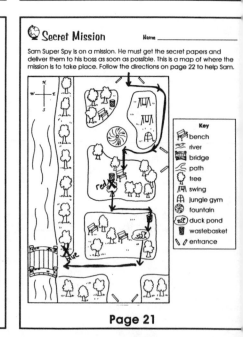

Key
- bench
- river
- bridge
- path
- tree
- swing
- jungle gym
- fountain
- duck pond
- wastebasket
- entrance

Page 21

Find It There

Name _____

To find your way around a town or city you can use a street map. It shows the names of the streets.

Find the bookstore on the map. Now find it on the map. Look at the name of the street that goes past the bookstore. If you want to go to the bookstore, you will have to go to Smelt Street.

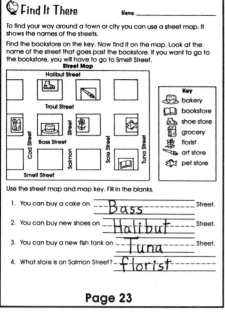

Use the street map and map key. Fill in the blanks.

1. You can buy a cake on __Bass__ Street.
2. You can buy new shoes on __Halibut__ Street.
3. You can buy a new fish tank on __Tuna__ Street.
4. What store is on Salmon Street? __Florist__

Page 23

At the Corner

Name _____

A street map shows how a town or city is divided into blocks. The corners of blocks are made when two streets cross each other. Use the street map to answer the questions.

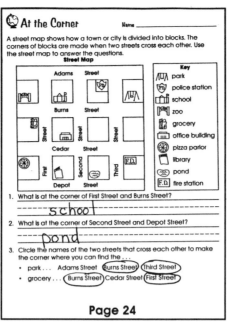

1. What is at the corner of First Street and Burns Street?
   __school__

2. What is at the corner of Second Street and Depot Street?
   __pond__

3. Circle the names of the two streets that cross each other to make the corner where you can find the . . .
   • park . . . Adams Street (Burns Street) (Third Street)
   • grocery . . . (Burns Street) Cedar Street (First Street)

Page 24

Just a Few Blocks

Name _____

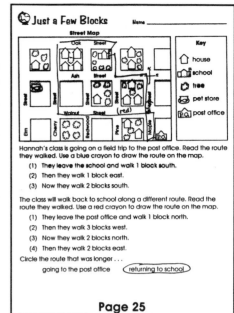

Hannah's class is going on a field trip to the post office. Read the route they walked. Use a blue crayon to draw the route on the map.

(1) They leave the school and walk 1 block south.
(2) Then they walk 1 block east.
(3) Now they walk 2 blocks south.

The class will walk back to school along a different route. Read the route they walked. Use a red crayon to draw the route on the map.

(1) They leave the post office and walk 1 block north.
(2) Then they walk 3 blocks west.
(3) Now they walk 2 blocks north.
(4) Finally, they walk 2 blocks east.

Circle the route that was longer . . .
   going to the post office   (returning to school)

Page 25

You're Invited

Name _____

Liz sent out invitations to her birthday party. She drew a map to show how to go from school to her house. Write north, south, east, or west and the street name to complete the sentences.

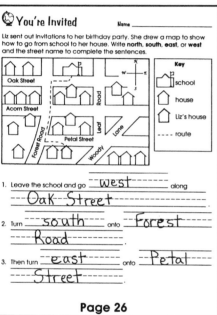

1. Leave the school and go __west__ along __Oak Street__

2. Turn __south__ onto __Forest Road__

3. Then turn __east__ onto __Petal Street__

Page 26

Ice Cream!

Name _____

Ding – Ding – Ding-a-ling! Here comes the ice-cream truck. On hot summer days, Stan drives his ice-cream truck around the neighborhood. He takes the same route every day. This map shows the neighborhood where Stan drives. Follow the directions on page 28.

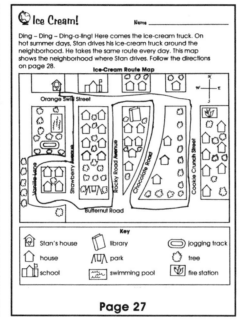

Page 27

Places to Go

Name _____

Mrs. Nelson needs to do many errands this afternoon. She only has a short time in which to do everything. Read Mrs. Nelson's list of things to do. Use the street map, map key, and symbols to answer the questions.

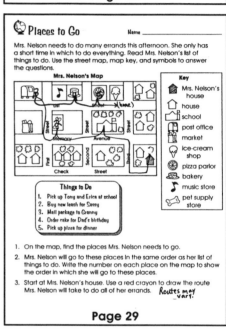

1. On the map, find the places Mrs. Nelson needs to go.
2. Mrs. Nelson will go to these places in the same order as her list of things to do. Write the number on each place on the map to show the order in which she will go to these places.
3. Start at Mrs. Nelson's house. Use a red crayon to draw the route Mrs. Nelson will take to do all of her errands. Routes may vary.

Page 29

Go the Distance

Name _____

This map shows the route for the yearly Pedalville Bike-a-thon. At the bottom of the map is a scale. A map scale helps you measure distance on a map.

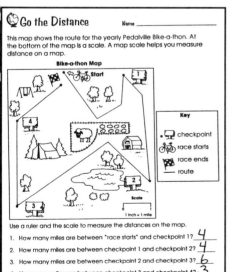

Use a ruler and the scale to measure the distances on the map.

1. How many miles are between "race starts" and checkpoint 1? __4__
2. How many miles are between checkpoint 1 and checkpoint 2? __4__
3. How many miles are between checkpoint 2 and checkpoint 3? __6__
4. How many miles are between checkpoint 3 and checkpoint 4? __3__
5. How many miles are between checkpoint 4 and "race ends"? __2__

Page 30

Are We There Yet?

Name _____

using a map scale

Calvin is going on a vacation to Getaway Campground. Use the scale and a ruler to answer the questions below.

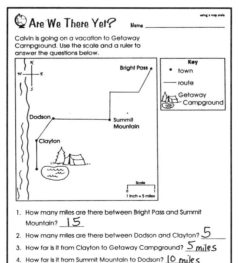

1. How many miles are there between Bright Pass and Summit Mountain? __15__
2. How many miles are there between Dodson and Clayton? __5__
3. How far is it from Clayton to Getaway Campground? __5 miles__
4. How far is it from Summit Mountain to Dodson? __10 miles__
5. How many miles are in all are there between Bright Pass and Getaway Campground? __35__

Page 31

Hot Air Balloon Race

Name _____

It's the Grand Hot Air Balloon Race. Use the map scale and a ruler to find out how far the hot air balloons will travel each day of the race.

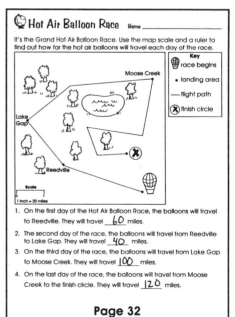

1. On the first day of the Hot Air Balloon Race, the balloons will travel to Reedville. They will travel __60__ miles.
2. The second day of the race, the balloons will travel from Reedville to Lake Gap. They will travel __40__ miles.
3. On the third day of the race, the balloons will travel from Lake Gap to Moose Creek. They will travel __100__ miles.
4. On the last day of the race, the balloons will travel from Moose Creek to the finish circle. They will travel __120__ miles.

Page 32

Across the Line

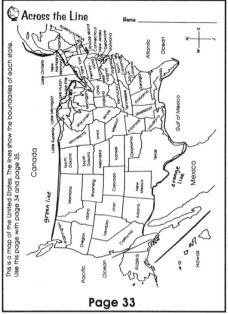

This is a map of the United States. The lines show the boundaries of each state. Use this page with page 34 and page 35.

Page 33

Across the Line (Continued)

Name _____

Use the United States map on page 33 to complete the following.

1. What is the name of the state in which you live? *Answers will vary.*

2. Draw a blue line along the boundary lines of the state where you live.

3. What country is north of the United States?

   Canada

4. Draw a green line along the boundary between the United States and Canada.

5. What country is south of the United States?

   Mexico

6. Draw an orange line along the southern boundary of the United States.

7. Find the state, country, or body of water that is the . . .

   northern boundary of your state. Color it green.

   eastern boundary of your state. Color it blue.

   southern boundary of your state. Color it yellow.

   western boundary of your state. Color it red.

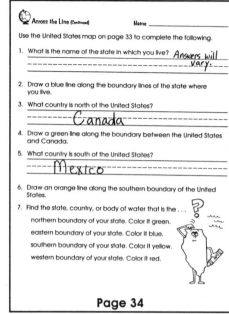

Page 34

Crossing the States

Name _____

Use the map of the United States on page 33 and the compass rose to fill in the puzzle.

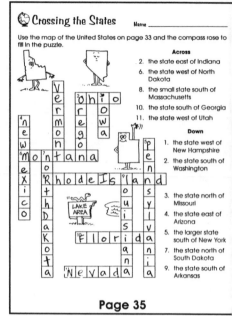

Across

2. the state east of Indiana
6. the state west of North Dakota
8. the small state south of Massachusetts
10. the state south of Georgia
11. the state west of Utah

Down

1. the state west of New Hampshire
2. the state south of Washington
3. the state north of Missouri
4. the state east of Arizona
5. the larger state south of New York
7. the state north of South Dakota
9. the state south of Arkansas

Page 35

Water Watch

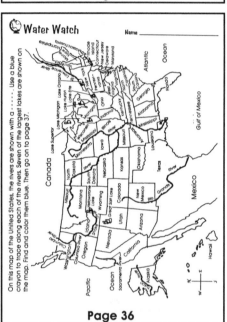

On this map of the United States, the rivers are shown with a - - - -. Use a blue crayon to trace along each of the rivers. Seven of the largest lakes are shown on the map. Find and color them blue. Then go on to page 37.

Page 36

Water Watch (Continued)

Name _____

Use the map on page 36 to find the answers to the questions.

1. The lakes along the northern border of the United States are called the Great Lakes. Write the names of these five lakes.

   Lake Superior, Lake Michigan, Lake Huron, Lake Erie, Lake Ontario

2. Which river flows along the border between Canada and the United States?

   St. Lawrence River

3. What is the name of the lake in Utah?

   Great Salt Lake

4. Which river flows along the border between Washington and Oregon?

   Columbia River

5. Circle the name of the river that flows along the border between Mexico and the United States.

   Mississippi River   (Rio Grande River)   Yukon River   Missouri River

6. Circle the name of the river that flows through the state of Alaska.

   Mississippi River   Rio Grande River   (Yukon River)   Missouri River

7. How many states does the Mississippi River flow through or past?

   10

Page 37

What a Vacation!

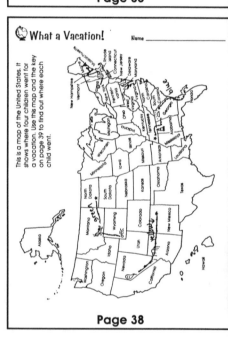

This is a map of the United States. It shows where four children went for a vacation. Use this map and the key on page 39 to find out where each child went.

Page 38

What a Vacation! (Continued)

Name _____

Key

- ➤➤➤ David's trip
- •••• Becky's trip
- ---- Adam's trip
- ---- Sheila's trip
- ★ home
- National Baseball Hall of Fame and Museum
- Fossil Butte National Monument
- Dahlonega Gold Museum
- Sea World
- Grand Canyon
- U.S. Space and Rocket Center
- Grasshopper Glacier
- Basketball Hall of Fame
- Virginia City (old mining town)

1. Use a yellow crayon to trace David's route.
2. Use a blue crayon to trace Becky's route.
3. Use a red crayon to trace Adam's route.
4. Use a green crayon to trace Sheila's route.

5. Which person probably likes sports?   Adam
6. Which person traveled the farthest west?   David
7. Which person traveled the farthest south?   Becky
8. Write the names of the places Sheila went to see on her vacation.

   Grasshopper Glacier
   Fossil Butte National Monument

9. Where did Becky go in Florida?

   Sea World

Page 39

Within Continents

Name _____

This map shows two continents and two oceans. It also shows the countries that are on each continent. A solid line (———) shows the boundaries of each country. Use this map to answer the questions on page 44.

Page 43

Within Continents (Continued)

Name _____

1. Write the names of the continents shown on the map.

   North America
   South America

2. Find the United States on the map. Color it green.
3. Find Alaska and Hawaii. They are part of the country of the United States. Color them green.
4. What country is north of the United States? Color it orange.

   Canada

5. What large country is south of the United States? Color it red.

   Mexico

6. Which South American country is the biggest?

   Brazil

7. What long, skinny country is on the west coast of South America?

   Chile

8. Which ocean is to the west of the continents of North America and South America?

   Pacific

9. In which direction would you go to travel from Canada to Chile?

   South

Page 44

IF5189 Map Skill